Original title:
The Grapes of Eternity

Copyright © 2025 Creative Arts Management OÜ
All rights reserved.

Author: Charles Whitfield
ISBN HARDBACK: 978-1-80586-272-7
ISBN PAPERBACK: 978-1-80586-744-9

Spellbound by the Harvest Moon

In a vineyard bright, where laughter flows,
Grapes sway like dancers, in rows they pose.
A barrel's a throne, a cork's a fine hat,
As vines whisper secrets, and giggle with fat.

The moon's shining down, a spotlight so grand,
Grapes plotting mischief, it's all quite unplanned.
With every sip taken, the stars seem to cheer,
As we toast to the night with our uproarious beer.

A grape on the loose, it's rolling away,
It dreams of a journey, a grand cabernet play.
Two bunches merging, one says, "You're my friend!"
"Let's ferment our dreams till the party won't end!"

Under the sky, with the laughter so bright,
We stomp on the grapes, oh what a delight!
With each squishy pop, we erupt into glee,
Creating fine chaos, just you wait and see!

Threads of the Past in Liquid Form

In a bottle, time does sway,
Laughing grapes from yesterday.
Spilled secrets on a tablecloth,
Their jokes, far too grand to scoff.

Sipping tales of love and woe,
Where mischief begins to flow.
A cork pops with awkward cheer,
As history bends with a sneer.

Elysian Delights

Beneath a sun that fumbles bright,
Fruits conspire to tease the night.
A cluster giggles, plump and round,
While shadows dance on grassy ground.

The juice of laughter spills sublime,
What a vintage sense of rhyme!
Each sip a laugh, each bite a grin,
Life's silliness tucked within.

Chorus of the Untouched Fields

In untouched rows where breezes play,
The vines hum tunes of yesterday.
A band of greens with rhythm tight,
Twirling leaves beneath starlight.

They serenade the buzzing bees,
With off-key notes carried by the breeze.
In perfect harmony they sway,
Mocking time in their own way.

Shadows of Yesterday's Clusters

Shadows linger; they cling with glee,
Remembering grape escapades, you see.
They tell of fights with the wind's embrace,
And whispers of love from a boozy place.

In the refrains of dusk they shout,
"Who squished us here? Let's work it out!"
With every stomp and stomp in jest,
These shadows laugh—oh, what a fest!

A Tapestry of Seasons

In spring's bright light, we dance and play,
   Chasing blossoms that drift away.
  Summer's heat makes us quite wobbly,
    Ice cream melting, oh so sloppily.

  Autumn leaves, a crunchy delight,
Pumpkin spice makes everything right.
Winter comes, with snowflakes galore,
 We trip on sleds, then laugh even more.

Immortal Juice

In a bottle of dreams, a swirl of fate,
Grapes giggle softly, oh what a state!
Stomped by feet that sing a tune,
Creating nectar beneath the moon.

With each sip, a chuckle unfolds,
Tales of Vikings and knights of old.
Mad scientists mix with jelly beans,
Turning fizzy drinks into grape-filled machines.

Reflections in the Wine

In a glass so gleaming, we peer inside,
Tiny fairies dance, they just can't hide.
Each swirl is a story, a giggle or two,
Puns and hiccups in every brew.

A sip brings forth laughter of past and present,
While corks pop like jokes, oh how pleasant!
A toast to the hapless, the joyful, the bold,
The clumsy yet charming, their tales retold.

The Last Sip of Existence

As the bottle empties, we ponder the end,
With one final sip, my dear drunken friend.
Laughter erupts over stories untold,
About grapes that wore crowns, and dreams made of gold.

So we raise our glasses, with joy and with cheer,
Sipping life's essence with nary a fear.
In vino veritas, they say with a wink,
We'll spill just a bit, but we'll never sink.

The Ripple of Time's Wine

In the cellar of dreams where the oddities flow,
Bottles whisper secrets, they don't want to show.
A cork pops a joke, bubbles rise with a grin,
The flavor of laughter, where mischief begins.

Chardonnay ducks in a tiptoe parade,
While Merlot winks at the clumsy charade.
Pinot grigio spills all its grape-colored tea,
While spirits beguile in this party for free.

The barrel laughs softly, it's been here a while,
Aged wisdom of pranks hidden under its smile.
As wine stains the tablecloth, hues of delight,
Time sips on the antics beneath the moonlight.

Currents of the Unseen Past

In a river of giggles, the timeline flows,
Historical hiccups, the truth no one knows.
A caveman with wine stains and a laugh that won't cease,

Painting portraits of folly, a canvas of peace.

Wandering winks from a jester's old jest,
Tangled in stories that always digress.
Ancient grapes roll, with a tumble and pun,
Chasing the shadows where daylight has spun.

The rivers of time swirl with childish delight,
As echoes of laughter dance into the night.
A wise old oak chuckles, it's seen it all,
While the current keeps laughing, both small and tall.

Festivities of Forever

Under the boughs where the fiestas ignite,
Grapes are the dancers, full of delight.
They twirl through the air, with a zestful delight,
Making merriment rise, a whimsical sight.

The starlight's a witness to this bubbly spree,
As the moon takes a sip from the laughing spree.
Sangria serenades the platters of cheer,
While the fruitcake frets, 'Am I too severe?'

Goblins and fairies prance wildly around,
While laughter and joy are eternally found.
In the fest of forever, where fun takes a stand,
Every moment is fleeting, yet perfectly planned.

Tendrils of Memory

In the garden of memory, vines twist and turn,
Where laughter blooms gently, and funny tales churn.
A grape in a top hat begins to recite,
The fables of folly under soft twilight.

With each sip of sweetness, more giggles arise,
A sprinkle of mischief hidden in the skies.
Tendrils of time reach for whimsical tastes,
While clowns ride on chariots made out of grapes.

An old memory trips on the roots of the past,
And tumbles in merriment, hoping to last.
Each tendril tickles, a reminder to play,
As laughter and memories mingle each day.

Echoes of the Endless Orchard

In a grove where giggles grow,
Fruits wear hats and put on shows.
A squirrel juggles with a pear,
While chickens dance without a care.

The moon swings low, a merry sight,
As stars take turns to play all night.
Beneath the branches, laughter beams,
In this orchard of absurd dreams.

A Feast for the Celestial Palate

A table set with cosmic pies,
The pudding winks and starts to rise.
Galaxies swirl in rainbow bowls,
Munching on stardust, filling souls.

A comet cooks, with spices grand,
While planets serve on silver sand.
With every bite, the cosmos sings,
A feast where joy is king of things.

Gathering Stars from Forgotten Fields

In fields where time has lost its race,
We gather twinkles, every trace.
With baskets made of lunar light,
We pluck the stars on this fine night.

A dancing cloud polishes the sun,
While shadows giggle, just for fun.
Each star we gather tells a joke,
As constellations start to poke.

Fruit of the Cosmic Nebula

From pulpy clouds, the nectar drips,
With fruit that bounces on our lips.
Black holes burp and chuckle loud,
In this laughter, we are cowed.

Asteroids play hopscotch in the air,
Comets join in without a care.
The fruit we taste is odd and bright,
Yet tickles hearts with pure delight.

Tales from the Orchard of Forever

In an orchard grand, with trees so wide,
Fruits hang low, on branches they glide.
A squirrel in shades, sipping on juice,
Says, "Life's a party! Let's cut loose!"

Cherries giggle, pears dance in line,
While apples complain, "This isn't divine!"
The wind whispers jokes, leaves flap in glee,
As laughter rings out, from each fruitful tree.

Pondering the Age of Twisting Vines

Vines twist and turn, in a dizzying spree,
Hoping to win, a vine-wrapping tea.
They prance like dancers, with roots in the ground,
Shouting, "We're funky! Come join us around!"

A grape with a mustache rolls down the lane,
Claiming, "I'm vintage, not quite the same!"
The sun breaks a grin, the clouds start to sway,
"Who knew a vine could sillily play?"

The Elixir of the Endless Seasons

Bottles of laughter, aged to perfection,
Sip from my glass, spark joy's reflection.
Bubbles like dreams, effervescent and bright,
"Who needs a plan? Let's party all night!"

Each sip, a giggle, a tickle on tongues,
As fruit fables blossom where no one's sprung.
The cork pops with cheer, dreams flow like the breeze,
Old tales are reborn, if you just pour with ease.

Labyrinths of Aromatic Timelessness

In a maze of scents, I tangled my nose,
Roses with raspberries, oh how it goes!
A whiff of wild laughter, a taste of sweet cheer,
Lost in the fragrance, where giggles draw near.

Leaves whisper secrets, as petals conspire,
To brew mischievous tales wrapped in desire.
The clock turns awry, time takes a nap,
Dancing with aromas, in a magical lap.

Elixir of the Ages

In a jar of joy, I found my way,
Odd concoctions lead me astray.
Laughter bubbles, a sweet delight,
Sip and grin, oh what a sight!

In the market, the bottles gleam,
Labelled 'Magic' – could it be a dream?
A wobbly walk, a giggle or two,
I dance like a chicken, yes, it's true!

Old recipes with a silly twist,
Potion brews you shouldn't miss.
With every taste, I feel so free,
Elixirs made for you and me!

So raise your glass, let laughter ring,
For every drop, a joke we bring.
In this happy sip, we all belong,
Join the fun, let's sing along!

Shadows of the Timeless Orchard

In the orchard where shadows prance,
The fruits giggle, a funny dance.
Apples whisper secrets wide,
While pears roll over, filled with pride.

A scarecrow thinks it's all a show,
But the pumpkins know he's just too slow.
With every breeze, the branches sway,
Tickling fruits in a playful way.

Beneath the trees, the squirrels conspire,
Hiding treasures, they never tire.
With cheeky grins and nimble feet,
They challenge everyone for a treat!

As sunset drapes its golden hue,
The orchard sings a funny tune.
With laughter spilling from every vine,
Join the shadows, it's harvest time!

Secrets in Each Blossom

In the garden, secrets bloom,
Petals giggle, fragrance loom.
Daisies tell a sneaky joke,
While tulips dance and gently poke.

A bee buzzes with a wacky tale,
Of how he once tried to ride a whale.
In each blossom, life is bold,
Spilling secrets, never old.

Butterflies chat in colors bright,
Trading stories, taking flight.
With every flutter, chuckles soar,
Nature's humor, we adore!

So stop and sniff, don't be shy,
Each blossom holds a laugh nearby.
As petals sway in breezy returns,
Life's little secrets, everyone learns!

Twilight's Sweet Harvest

Twilight falls, the feast begins,
Fruits chuckle as daylight thins.
With baskets full and spirits high,
The stars all twinkle and sigh.

Cherries chat with a sense of glee,
"Pick me, pucker, just wait and see!"
Ripe and ready, they get their chance,
As moonlight leads a funny dance.

Under the moon, we raise a cheer,
For each sweet bite, shed every fear.
Laughter rings through the soft, cool night,
Harvesting joy, what a sight!

With every fruit, a giggle shared,
Twilight's harvest, perfectly paired.
So gather 'round, let worries fade,
In this sweet twilight, let laughter cascade!

Cycles of Growth and Decay

In the garden, worms do prance,
Chasing shadows, seeking chance.
Flowers bloom and then they fade,
Life's a game of charades made.

Roots entwined with giggles low,
Underneath, the secrets flow.
Leaves fall down like confetti bright,
Nature plays with pure delight.

Buds appear like hopeful dreams,
Nature laughs, or so it seems.
Turn around, and see them spin,
Life's a dance where all can win.

From the ground, a chuckle sighs,
As the dried leaves wave goodbyes.
Yet here, in this merry fray,
Cycles turn with fun at play.

Fragments of Eternal Seasons

Winter slips on a banana peel,
While summer grills a noisy meal.
Springtime giggles, cracks some jokes,
As autumn dances with the folks.

Snowmen melt in cheerful glee,
Waving hats from the old pine tree.
Summer's sun wears shades at night,
Just to keep the mood so light.

Leaves play games of peek-a-boo,
As wind whispers secrets new.
Seasons juggle, round they go,
Creating laughs in nature's show.

In this cycle, time's a tease,
Tickling trees with playful breeze.
Fragments tossed in whimsy's spin,
Nature knows, let the fun begin!

Jewels of the Cosmic Garden

Stars like grapes hang in the sky,
Winking down as if to pry.
While comets race to steal a bite,
In the garden of pure delight.

Galaxies, like flowers, twirl,
Spinning 'round a cosmic whirl.
Planets strut with shiny hats,
Chatting softly, "What of that?"

Stardust sprinkles laughter bright,
Crafting dreams throughout the night.
In this garden, wild and free,
Space is filled with joyful glee.

Planets swing in merry chase,
Grinning wide in this great space.
Jewels drift in cosmic cheer,
Nature's fun, forever here!

Strains of a Timeless Heart

Beats of laughter, echoes fly,
Tickling hearts that float on by.
With each thud, a playful jest,
Life's a game, a merry quest.

Melodies loop like a tape,
As wishes dance and dreams escape.
Whispers of love in tones so sweet,
Turn the mundane to a treat.

In the rhythm, joys collide,
Filling gaps with smiles wide.
Echoing through the boundless night,
A timeless heart keeps spirits light.

Strains of mirth in every beat,
Life's a song that can't be beat.
Melodies swirl, together part,
In every note, a joyful heart.

Sipping on the Essence of Forever

In a glass of dreams, we pour,
Bubbles dance like never before.
Laughter spills, a fizzy cheer,
Time skips like a jester, here.

Grapes of wisdom, oh so bold,
Legends shared, both new and old.
Sips of joy, with every cheer,
Losing track of our own year.

Sunshine spritzes every drop,
With funny faces, we won't stop.
A toast to silly, wild delight,
In this nectar, we're all right.

So raise your glass, let worries flee,
In this moment, we're completely free.
Forever's just a laugh away,
In this essence, let's forever play.

The Vineyard Beyond the Horizon

In a land where grapes take flight,
They wear top hats, what a sight!
Waltzing vines in evening glow,
Sipping dreams, let's steal the show.

Grapes gossip under the sun,
Tickling leaves, oh what a pun!
They whisper secrets from the past,
In their laughter, joy is cast.

Clusters hanging, silly sway,
Waving hello, 'come join our play!'
With every twist of vine so bright,
We chase the stars through the night.

So come, my friend, let's take a stroll,
Through the fields, give life our whole.
In the vineyard, laughter rings,
With every sip, our hearts take wings.

Nectar of the Unfathomable Night

In the shadows, whispers tease,
Drink this nectar, take your ease.
Moonlight giggles on the tongue,
As silly songs are softly sung.

Jars of laughter, filled to the brim,
Under a sky that's never grim.
Stars bark orders, grapes salute,
Sipping joy in a silly suit.

With every sip, we lose our way,
In this night, we're all ballet.
Twisting and twirling 'round the glow,
The silliness just can't be low.

So chase the dusk, let's taste delight,
In this nectar, we're weightless, light.
Forever's just a punchline away,
In the humor of the night, we sway.

Roots Entwined with Infinity

With roots so deep, we dance and play,
Bound by laughter, come what may.
Wiggling roots share silly tales,
While tickled vines blow gentle gales.

Underneath the soil, we jest,
Finding fun, we never rest.
Worms tell stories, grapes laugh loud,
Creating chaos, oh so proud.

Twisting together, grapes agree,
Infinity's just fun, you see.
With every sip and hearty cheer,
Together forever, we persevere.

So let's entwine, grow wild and free,
In this bond, just you and me.
We're roots of humor, come align,
Forever's bright in this sweet vine.

Embers of the Infinite Harvest

In a vineyard of laughter, the vines sway,
Dancing like they've won a silly ballet.
Grapes wear hats made of foil and twine,
Sipping on sunshine, feeling divine.

The sun tickles leaves, making them giggle,
While clowns with red noses do a little wiggle.
In this vineyard, joy grows on each vine,
With every drop of dew, it tastes so fine.

A grape slipped a note in a bottle of wine,
Said, "Don't worry, buddy, we'll all be just fine!"
With grape juice smiles, they bounce to the beat,
Offering laughter, so fruity and sweet.

As barrels roll by, like ships on a spree,
The harvest is full of pure jubilee.
With bottles uncorked, the jesters all cheer,
To the comedic fruit, we raise a big beer!

Chasing Sunlight through Eternal Canopies

Underneath shade where laughter can thrive,
Grapes play hide and seek, oh, how they strive!
Sunlight peeks through with a tickling touch,
The vines whisper secrets, oh, so much.

A squirrel snickers, wearing grape-shaped glasses,
Watching the grapes as they trip on their classes.
"You must be blushing, you cheeky little bunch!"
They giggle and roll, oh what a fun crunch!

With a breeze that hums tunes from days gone past,
They sway and they sway, their shadows they cast.
In a world where both silliness reigns supreme,
Each cluster's a note in a whimsical dream.

And when the sky's painted with twilight's blush,
They've raced the sun's rays in a sweet, silly rush.
Grapes chase the night, the stars burst in delight,
While laughter and joy dance on the edge of night!

Whispers of Time in Gilded Bunches

In a field where giggles sprout like fine wine,
Gilded bunches of grapes form a long, silly line.
They whisper sweet tales of their merry old fate,
"We're the ones to toast to—just don't be late!"

With shoes made of leaves, they prance and they leap,
Making time sound funny, not a second to keep.
Each laugh is a drop in the grape's juicy jest,
In the realm of the harvest, they all are the best.

The clock strikes a tune, in a merry quick dance,
While grapes don top hats and waltz in romance.
A bottle rolls by, laughing loud in the sun,
"Who knew that our harvest would be so much fun?"

As twilight arrives, they gather in cheer,
With bubbles in glasses, they banish all fear.
For time is a jester, and funny it seeks,
In the world of these grapes, laughter freely speaks!

When the Moon Dances in Crystalline Clusters

When the moon beams down with a mischievous grin,
The grapes all gather for a nocturnal spin.
Crystalline clusters twinkle like stars,
Telling moonlit jokes about their grape-y memoirs.

Under the starlight, the vines twist and sway,
Giggling softly in their own funny way.
A fairy drops by with a gleam in her eye,
"Who knew grapes could party? Oh my, oh my!"

With shadows that dance and shimmer so bright,
These fruity companions love the soft night.
They hum little tunes, full of laughter and cheer,
Making the darkness just a shade less severe.

So raise up your glasses to the moon's silly light,
To grapes in the moonbeams, everything feels right.
For when clusters unite under stars and the sky,
The harvest of humor will never run dry!

Blossoms of Forgotten Futures

In a garden, grapes wear hats,
Dancing squirrels host chitchat.
The sun tickles the vine's embrace,
While daisies giggle in this space.

Once a grape dreamed to be fine wine,
But tripped and fell on marzipan twine.
Now rolling 'round, it takes a break,
Flavors mingle in a grape-filled lake.

Locusts play cards with the bumblebees,
Debating who's the best at cheese.
Ripe tomatoes try to show their might,
But cucumber jokes steal the spotlight.

Each bud whispers tales of old,
Of laughter shared and dreams retold.
A mischievous wind blows through the place,
And suddenly, it's a grape gala race!

The Vineyard Beyond the Veil

Where shadows sip on lemon tea,
Grapes dressed in velvet, full of glee.
They chat with ghosts over sips of zest,
While mischievous sprites never let them rest.

Here, the grapes wear tiny frowns,
Conspiring against the muddy clowns.
One grape yelled, 'Hey, let's take flight!'
But the pumpkin said, 'Not without a fight!'

A snail in glasses reads the news,
As dandelions sport polka-dot shoes.
They argue who gets the nicest view,
But all they see is the cows mooing too.

The moonlight chuckles on the leaves,
As grape vines twine like playful thieves.
In a world of fruits where laughter swells,
They toast their health with fizzy spells!

Harmony of the Everfruit

In a land of whimsy and bright delight,
Fruits unite for a dance at night.
Bananas slip on grape skins galore,
While melons bust out a jig on the floor.

A fruity band plays catchy beats,
With apples tapping their tiny feet.
The owls hoot in rhythm, so wise and sly,
As citrus-folk dream of a pie in the sky.

Berries argue about their sweet fame,
While peaches shout, 'Hey, don't steal my name!'
But all is well, as they find their groove,
In this funny fruit fest, they can't help but move.

With laughter ringing under the stars,
They toss confetti from tiny jars.
And in this revelry, joy takes root,
As they sing to the tune of the old fruit flute.

Labors of the Unyielding Soil

In fields where dirt wears a plaid suit,
Frogs chant songs of hard-rooted fruit.
The turnips joke about getting pulled,
While cabbages wait, their plans all dulled.

Grapes fret, 'Will we ever be wine?
Or just a joke in a cornfield line?'
As the soil chuckles, warm and deep,
It quickens the dreams that the harvest keeps.

Ants form bands with a bold decree,
We'll work hard, not just for tea!
But when the cloaked gopher shows his face,
The crops all tremble, their fears embrace.

Yet still they toil, with heart and glee,
In the hopes that someday they will see,
The fruits of laughter grow from the ground,
In this funny garden where joy is found.

Ode to the Unyielding Grape

In the sun, they hang like troops,
Mocking us with endless loops.
Squished and pressed, but still they smile,
In a dance that lasts a while.

With every pour, they twist and whirl,
The grapevine hosts a silly twirl.
"Drink up!" they say, with frothy cheer,
As we indulge their juicy sphere.

Sweet and sour, a playful jest,
In every bottle, they find rest.
But when we sip, watch out for spills,
Those tiny pearls have mischievous wills.

In the end, they're quite sublime,
Entwined in laughter, grapes in rhyme.
Raise your glass, let's toast tonight,
To these jesters, pure delight!

The Timeless Vineyard's Lament

Among the vines, the whispers flow,
"Why do you drink? It's all for show!"
Yet here we sip, like it's our fate,
These grapey giggles we celebrate.

The rows of green begin to sway,
As we sip more, they start to play.
"Join us!" they chime, with all their might,
It turns the day into a night.

Oh, vintage dreams, so sly and bold,
Chasing shadows, stories told.
"Another round?" they slyly wink,
In every swig, we lose our blink.

With frolicking vines that tease and poke,
They spill their secrets, oh what a joke!
In faded barrels, laughter hides,
And timeless tales tie up our guides.

Bottled Memories in the Grove

In every cork, a tale is told,
Of summer suns and nights so bold.
A pop, a fizz, we raise a cheer,
To bottled memories, far and near.

The labels label all our glee,
"Drink responsibly!" they plead with me.
But in good fun, who can resist?
This liquid joy we all persist.

Grapes in barrels gossip deep,
While we pretend, we're not in heap.
With every drop, a laughter spark,
In light of moon or in the dark.

So here's to nights that never fade,
And sips like treasures, nicely laid.
In leafy groves where dreams collide,
We bottle joy, no need to hide.

Dreams Fermented Under Stars

Beneath the sky, we raise our glass,
To fermented dreams that come to pass.
With cheeky grapes that laugh away,
The troubles of our busy day.

Stars twinkle bright, a vintage spree,
"Join us, dear friend, come drink with me!"
As we toast to midnight's playful fray,
These fleeting dreams won't slip away.

The moonlit vines sway back and forth,
Spitting puns of grape-like worth.
And every sip leads to a grin,
As laughter swirls where joy begins.

So let us dance with shades of red,
And sip the cheer, let worries shed.
Beneath these stars, the night feels right,
In dreams fermented, we take flight.

Dancing Shadows in Eternal Breezes

In twilight's glow, shadows prance,
Beneath the stars, they twist and dance.
With giggles bright, they tell their tales,
Of slipping sandals and ghostly gales.

The moonlight yields to playful jest,
As laughter fills the evening's quest.
A waltz of leaves, a jive of light,
Where everything's wrong yet feels so right.

They tiptoe 'round the grapevine wraps,
In capes made of dandelion traps.
With every sip of cosmic wine,
They toast to dreams that intertwine.

In breezes bold, their secrets spin,
While crickets join the dance within.
So raise a cup and let it flow,
In whimsical ways, where shadows grow.

Chronicles of the Infinite Harvest

Once upon a vine's bold tale,
Where fruit wore hats and danced in sale.
A berry bright, with cheeky grin,
Said, 'Come on, let the fun begin!'

With baskets full of laughter's might,
They gathered high in sheer delight.
The squash wore shades, the carrots pranced,
In the merry fray, no veggie chanced.

Each harvest ripe, a joke in tow,
Cabbages giggle, corn does flow.
With hands in pockets, they play charades,
Under the sun, like grand parades.

Feuds of peas in playful brawl,
As radish friends just wanted ball.
Chronicles of the garden bloom,
In joyful chaos, life's sweet perfume.

The Secrets of the Celestial Vineyard

In celestial realms of jolly glee,
A vineyard twirls where stars run free.
With comets dressed in velvet hues,
Corked surprises, laughter ensues.

Whispers float through nebulae's sighs,
Where constellations swap their ties.
The grapes, they giggle, keeping score,
Of every jest from yonder shore.

A bottle lands, a twist, a pop,
Celestial wine that makes hearts hop.
In cups of stardust, cheer's the tone,
Where silly secrets dance alone.

So raise a glass to cosmic cheer,
With every drop, the giggles near.
In galaxies vast, we'll toast tonight,
To fruity mischief, pure delight.

Horizon's Embrace in Lush Abundance

At dawn's first light, the giggles ring,
A horizon wide, let the humor spring.
With fields aglow and sunbeams bright,
Where every laugh is pure sunlight.

Abundant moments dressed in green,
With playful blooms, a sight unseen.
Tomatoes wink from leafy thrones,
While daisies toss their cheeky tones.

In laughter's chase, the wind does sway,
As the harvest tells a witty play.
A song of joy in nature's feast,
Where every bite is whimsy's least.

So gather 'round in this embrace,
Where fun and mirth fill every space.
With every sip and every cheer,
Life's grand banquet draws us near.

The Orchard's Eternal Heartbeat

In a quirky orchard where shadows play,
The fruits wear hats, come out to sway.
They laugh and giggle, their colors bright,
Dancing with glee through day and night.

Squirrels hold parties in the trees,
Bouncing around with the greatest of ease.
With acorn confetti and juice galore,
They toast to the harvest, then crave some more.

The apples joke, "We're so divine!"
"Let's brew a potion, with flavor so fine!"
The pears chime in, "And let's play a game,
We're the fairest in all, and we're never the same!"

So join the fun, take a stroll,
Through a merry garden, where laughter's the goal.
Every blossom whispers, 'Come have a slice!'
In the orchard's heart, where joy is precise.

Bounty of a Timeless Harvest

Once upon a vine, the grapes conspired,
To cloud the village, they almost retired.
"Let's roll away, let's have some fun!"
And so they tumbled, one by one.

The zucchini wore monocles, quite absurd,
While carrots shared sonnets, unheard.
The tomatoes tossed jokes that were ripe,
Tickling the senses, just as they'd hype.

Old potato decided to spin,
Whirling the turnips with a cheeky grin.
They danced in a circle, all in delight,
Claiming they'd stay till the morning light.

With laughter and cheer in every corner,
The harvest had turned into a foreigner.
So raise a toast to the timeless affair,
In this goofy garden, find joy everywhere!

Rays of Infinite Bloom

Underneath the sun, daisies boast,
"We're the best blooms, let's make a toast!"
The lilacs add, in a velvety style,
"With scents so divine, we'll make you smile!"

The sunflowers wore sunglasses, oh so cool,
"Join us for lunch, we'll feast by the pool!"
With snacks like sunshine and nectar divine,
They bragged about rays that warmed every vine.

Bumblebees buzzed, they led the fun,
"Let's gather all flowers, let's run!"
With petals a-flutter, they painted the air,
In a kaleidoscope of colors, without a care.

So here's to the blooms, to laughter and light,
With every petal, a smile in sight.
As seasons may change, and the world may zoom,
The rays of joy shine in every bloom!

Unfading Blossoms

In a garden of dreams where giggles soar,
The blooms wear spectacles and beg for more.
They chatter and gleam, with petals so bright,
Whispering tales till the fall of night.

The roses recite poetry, with flair so grand,
While the tulips juggle, as they take a stand.
Daffodils chuckle, playing tricks on the air,
Sprinkling their joy everywhere with flair.

Each bud is a joker, a prankster at heart,
Crafting delicious mischief, a true work of art.
With laughter like honey, they sweeten the day,
Proclaiming, "We'll bloom, come what may!"

So stroll through this realm where silliness grows,
In the land of unfading, where humor overflows.
For in every blossom and laugh that we share,
Lies an eternal spirit that floats in the air.

Lushness of the Infinite Fields

In fields where vapors waltz and twirl,
A fruit parade begins to whirl.
They giggle, dance with vines in chat,
Sipping sunshine in a hat.

Grapes, oh grapes, in cosmic jest,
Make wine from laughter, that's the best!
They plump and puff, so full of cheer,
Whispering secrets to the deer.

With rolly polly bugs in tow,
They juggle dreams, a stunning show.
The clouds wink down with cherry glee,
And toast to joys, just wait and see!

So raise a cup, toast high and bright,
To fruits that dance in sheer delight!
In vines of mirth, we find our bliss,
The world's our stage, what's not to miss!

Interstellar Grapes

On cosmic branches, fruits reside,
With stardust smiles and giggles wide.
They bounce through space, so free, so brave,
In comedy, they dig and wave.

A comet's tail, they ride in style,
With fruity flair, they span a mile.
They squeak and squawk, their voices loud,
Creating ripples in the crowd.

They've got the juice of ancient tales,
With cosmic puns and luck of snails.
From nebulae, they pluck a tune,
And rock the universe till noon!

So laugh with grapes from worlds unseen,
Where laughter reigns like splendid green.
In every sip, a burst of glee,
Interstellar joy, wild and free!

Nectar of the Boundless

In barrels large, the nectar glows,
A sugary laugh that always grows.
With honeyed humor, spills and spills,
Through every glass, it dances still.

The bees are buzzing, wearing shades,
Stirring sweet dreams in golden glades.
They sip the nectar, clap their hands,
Serenading sunlit lands.

With every drop, a giggle rings,
Of tipsy daisies and leather wings.
So come on down, don't be so shy,
Join in the laughter, let's all fly!

To sweeter days and fun in store,
With fruity tales that always soar.
In every bubble, joy compiles,
Nectar of laughter, that beguiles!

Echoes from the Vineyard

In vineyards rich, where echoes play,
The grapes are jesters, bright and gay.
They whisper jokes to passing breeze,
    Causing giggles in shady trees.

Puns roll and tumble down the lane,
As grapes conspire to crack the grain.
"They stomp our fables in a pot,
But hold your glass, we'll try a lot!"

With merry vines, they caper bold,
Sharing stories that never get old.
Their laughter bursts, a liquid cheer,
    A toast to moments we endear.

So raise your cup, let spirits soar,
In vineyards where the laughter's core.
The grapes are wisdom, mirth conveyed,
    Echoes sweet in twilight's shade.

Visions from the Timeless Aisle

In aisles where time forgot to flow,
I tripped on dreams and fruit on show.
The grapes wore hats, oh what a sight,
They joked and danced 'til the morning light.

A bottle rolled, it had a grin,
"Open me up, let the fun begin!"
I laughed so hard, I spilled my drink,
A berry winked, "Now, what do you think?"

The shelves were stacked with jests and puns,
As squirrels played chess under the buns.
Each sip a giggle, a friendly tease,
"Join our party; we'll aim to please!"

Time swayed like a vine in bloom,
As laughter echoed from the room.
With every twist, the vines would sing,
Life's a hoot; let the joy take wing!

A Journey through Fields of Everlasting Light

In fields where sunbeams love to snooze,
I stumbled on some silly snooze.
A rabbit chuckled, 'Don't go too fast!'
'These beams of light, they're quite the blast!'

The flowers giggled in colors bright,
As I pranced past, the dazzling sight.
Each step ignited footsteps' glee,
"Join our dance, oh come and be free!"

A lemonade stand made of clouds,
Served drinks to the laughter of crowds.
Each sip was a joke, a twist of fate,
"Try this one; it's truly great!"

With berries bouncing, making it fun,
The day rolled on like a race to run.
Under the sun, all worries flee,
In fields of light, just let it be!

Eternal Vines

In a vineyard vast where time stands still,
The grapes are grand; oh what a thrill!
They wear their crowns with such finesse,
Each pluck a laugh, who'd dare to guess?

Once I asked a vine for a tale,
"Should I wear shoes or just a veil?"
It giggled back, "Just take a sip,
And let the world give you a flip!"

As I strolled past, a berry cheered,
"Pour some sauce and we'll be steered!"
The vintage air filled with delight,
"Let's toast to dreams that feel just right!"

Days drift on like bubbles of wine,
With each cork popped, we intertwine.
In laughter's hold, forever we bind,
In this eternal grove, let joy unwind!

Whispers of the Infinite

A whisper swirled through endless rows,
"I'll tell you secrets that no one knows!"
The grapes, they winked and conspired loud,
"Join our feast; you'll feel so proud!"

A shadow leapt, a grape on the run,
"Catch me quick, let's have some fun!"
We raced through laughter, under bright skies,
The tales spun high like a kite that flies.

With giggles and hiccups the day unfurled,
Each sip a journey to a distant world.
"Stay here forever, don't even think,
Join the party, grab a drink!"

The echoes ring in this merry place,
As fruit and time made their embrace.
In whispers soft that float and sway,
We dance through night, and greet the day!

When Time Succumbs to Sweetness

In the vineyard where giggles grow,
Time skips a beat, don't you know?
Chasing dreams in grape-stained shoes,
Sipping laughter, we can't lose.

Unruly vines twist and twirl,
Each berry bursts with a whimsied swirl.
A tickle of juice, a splash of fun,
Time bows down as sweetness won.

The clock melts down like a ripe fruit,
Making mischief, oh what a hoot!
Whispers of joy in every sip,
When laughter's ripe, none can grip.

So raise your glass, let's make a toast,
To the sweetness we cherish the most.
In this silly bower, we shall play,
Where time succumbs to joy each day.

Boundless Nectar

Bouncing bottles on the shelf,
A hint of mischief, a joyful elf.
Nectar flows like laughter's song,
In this wild feast, we all belong.

Grinning fruits, hanging low,
Whispering secrets, a giggly show.
Stone and stem make merry tunes,
Raising cheer like dancing moons.

A splash of color, a wink so sly,
Gather 'round, let's share a high.
In this orchard where folly grows,
Boundless treasures, oh, how it glows!

So grab a grape, take a chance,
Join the fun of this frolicking dance.
Life's a party in every sip,
With boundless nectar that makes us flip!

Colors of the Eternal Harvest

In fields of laughter, colors blend,
Grapes of joy, our playful friend.
A rainbow spills from vine to vine,
Painting smiles with every wine.

Violet dreams and golden rays,
Twirling mockery of mundane days.
In this perennial spree, we cheer,
Sipping sunshine, drawing near.

Bubbly giggles burst like seeds,
The harvest blooms beyond our needs.
With every taste, a funny tale,
In hues of humor, we set sail.

So gather 'round, let's toast anew,
To the colors of life that feel so true.
With every glass, a wink and jest,
In this eternal harvest, we're blessed!

Provocations of the Infinite

Oh, the grapes that tease and play,
They whisper secrets in a cheeky way.
With every pluck, a chuckle wide,
In this vineyard, we take pride.

Unfurling vines like playful jesters,
Each bottle's cork, a daring tester.
They challenge time with fruity glee,
Insisting we laugh, just wait and see.

The skies above bring giggly fates,
As laughter ripens, and joy awaits.
A hint of mischief in every drop,
Provoking smiles that never stop.

So lift your glass, let merriment flow,
In this infinite jest where spirits glow.
With every sip, we find delight,
Provocations of joy, shining bright!

Adrift in Endless Vines

In a world where time seems to bend,
I stumbled on a vine, my dear friend.
It whispered secrets, draped in green,
My grapes were laughing, oh what a scene!

The sun was shining, a golden reel,
Tickling my toes, I twirled with zeal.
A wine jug danced, it tripped and fell,
And giggled out loud, under a spell!

Each fruit had stories of days gone by,
They chuckled and cracked, oh my, oh my!
But when I took a sip, what a surprise,
The giggles turned into grape-sized highs!

So here I sway on a vine so bold,
In this tipsy tale, you'll never grow old.
With friends in clusters, we'll toast the night,
With laughter and joy, oh what a sight!

Odes to Everlasting Clusters

In a vineyard where laughter is the rule,
Clusters of joy play the jester's fool.
With each burst of flavor, oh what a deal,
I laughed so hard, I could barely feel!

The corks popped off like fireworks bright,
Twinkling and tumbling, oh what a sight!
Each swirl in the glass, a merry parade,
Sipping the happiness, never to fade!

We danced with the bottles, in a grand ballet,
A waltz of the grapes, come join the fray!
They chuckled and shimmered, round and tight,
In this endless toast, all hearts took flight!

So let's raise a glass, to the vines and cheer,
For moments of bliss that draw us near.
In this playful land, forever we stay,
In odes of joy, let's sip the day!

Where Time Holds No Bounds

In a meadow where clocks simply don't tick,
The grapes tell jokes, oh what a trick!
With grapes dressed in bowties, they crack a pun,
While time rolls on, never to shun!

We juggle our dreams like barrels on hills,
Chasing sunsets that throw us some thrills.
With each pop of cork, laughter's the sound,
Where time holds no bounds, fun knows no round!

So join the grape ball, wear your best hat,
We'll cha-cha with clouds, how about that?
For in this realm, giggles spin round,
We pour out the joy until sleep's found!

Here in this garden, free as a kite,
Our spirits take flight, hearts shining bright.
Wherever we wander, in giggles we drown,
In a world so silly, we won't wear a frown!

The Wine of Forgotten Stars

In the night where the stars go to play,
Forgotten wishes sip wine by the bay.
They clink their glasses, a shimmery sight,
And share tales of old as they dance with delight!

With every deep swirl, secrets unfold,
Of dreamy escapades, both daring and bold.
The moon chuckles softly, keeps time with a grin,
As the laughter of stars serenades the din!

One star got tipsy, and fell from the sky,
"Hey, bring me a grape!" it giggled with sigh.
They tossed it a cluster, bright and divine,
And toasted to dreams over glasses of wine!

So let's chase the cosmos, with jokes that ignite,
With wine from the stars, we'll dance through the night.
For in this grand vineyard where laughter will flow,
We'll toast to forgotten stars and the joy they bestow!

Ephemeral Sips of Everlasting Light

In a vine of giggles, ripe and round,
I stumbled upon joy, trembling on the ground.
Bottled laughter, a potion quite divine,
Swirling with whimsy in every line.

The bottles are brimming with winks and grins,
But pop one open, and chaos begins!
A taste of delight, then a twist of fate,
I'm dancing on clouds with an odd-looking mate.

With hiccups of humor that swirl and bubble,
I sip on the giggles, forget all my trouble.
Beneath moonlit shimmers, we toast and we cheer,
To the sips of a night that tickles the ear!

An elixir of joy, oh so fleeting and fun,
Let's roll in the sweetness, just two under the sun!
Caught in this moment, I'll scream and I'll sigh,
For tomorrow, who knows? We might just fly high!

The Orchard of Celestial Memories

In an orchard of giggles, fruits hang so bright,
A banana that chuckles under the moonlight.
Cider of laughter spills over the ground,
Where memories of joy seem endlessly found.

Pick an apple, it giggles, a true prankster's scene,
With flavors of fun that sparkly and keen.
Twisted vines tangle, creating a mess,
Who knew fruits could make one feel so blessed?

Lemon zest laughter, so tangy, so bold,
Twirling and swirling, never growing old.
Underneath branches where gaffes come to play,
Who knew our harvest would lead us astray?

In this orchard of memories, sunlight will gleam,
With jests and with japes, we'll dance till we dream.
Let's sip on the joy that ripens with fun,
For laughter's the fruit, and we've only begun!

A Symphony of Infinite Thorns

A concert of giggles played on thorny strings,
Where laughter is wrapped in bizarre little flings.
With every note squeaky and pratfalls galore,
We're bumbling through melodies, begging for more.

Spike the punch with a cackle, let's raise the bar,
Each jest a crescendo, we're true rockstars!
Tangled in joy, oh, can't find my shoe,
Dancing through daisies, our laughter's the cue.

Though thorns may prick, we'll dodge and we'll weave,
In this symphony of frolic, how could we grieve?
With each uproarious verse, let's celebrate cheer,
For humor's the thicket where festivity's near.

Echoes of laughter, a chorus so bright,
We'll waltz through the night, till the morning's first light.

So tune in to the merriment, join in the fun,
For a thorny ensemble, has only begun!

Seeds of Time's Boundless Harvest

From seeds of giggles that sprout and unfurl,
We plant our tomfoolery, let laughter twirl.
Springs of silliness, with buds all around,
In gardens of folly, where joy can be found.

We water with whimsy, we prune with a tease,
Alluding to laughter like buzzing bees.
Harvesting chuckles in baskets so full,
Jump into the riot, let's break every rule!

Fruits of our labor, sweet jests on the vine,
Each bite brings a giggle, oh, look at that line!
A pie made of punchlines, with frosting of cheer,
Our banquet of mirth brings the whole world near.

With seeds of the silly, we'll flourish and bloom,
Creating a landscape that brightens the room.
So let's sow the laughter, till daylight is done,
For the harvest of humor has only begun!

Unwritten Flavors of Eternity

In a garden of whispers, we taste the air,
Each fruit is a riddle, a joke we must share.
Laughter bubbles up like a fizzy surprise,
With each silly wobble, we roll on our thighs.

Beneath leafy laughter, time ticks in disguise,
The berries giggle, the sunlight complies.
With bites that tickle, we smile and we twirl,
Eternity's flavors give life a good swirl.

A smoothie of moments, each sip is a song,
Where all of our follies—oh, they're never wrong.
We relish the sweetness, let hiccups abound,
In the orchard of nonsense, true joy can be found.

So grab your bright chalice, let's toast to the fun,
Because in this grand joke, we find we're all one.
With laughter as solace, we'll dance 'neath the sun,
In flavors of timelessness, we'll never be done.

Seeds of Yesterday's Dreams

Digging through dirt, we uncover our glee,
Each seed is a story, a wild jubilee.
We plant with abandon, our hopes start to sprout,
In the garden of whimsy, there's never a doubt.

The sun on our backs, like a tickling hand,
Watering with silliness, dreams bloom on demand.
Each cherry-red laugh, a fruit of our quest,
Yesterday's folly now grows with the rest.

In patches of giggles, we tend to our fate,
Who knew that our laughter would taste so great?
We harvest the moments as they tumble down,
Dancing like potatoes, in joy's golden gown.

Let's feast on our blunders, they're quite the delight,
To revel in mischief, we'll party all night.
With seeds of our dreams tucked tight in the ground,
We're gardeners of glee, where joy knows no bound.

Resonance of the Ancient Orchard

In the heart of the grove, the gnarled roots chuckle,
Where age-old legacies wear their best buckle.
The apples are jokers, all dressed up in skin,
With puns in their peels—let the laughter begin!

Sunbeams twinkling like mischievous sprites,
Whispering tales of our whimsical fights.
The pears bounce around in a comedic spin,
Where rustles of laughter invite us all in.

With crunches like cymbals, we munch with delight,
Each bite brings a giggle, from morning till night.
In this playful haven, where giggly trees sway,
We dance through the shadows, where silliness plays.

So come toss your worries on branches so high,
In orchards of mirth, we'll aim for the sky.
With echoes of joy that the ancients have known,
We feast on the laughter, a world of our own.

Embrace of the Unmortal

In a realm where the giggles dance ever sublime,
We hug the absurd, we embrace the lost time.
Where the clocks go to nap, and the rules take a break,
Each tick is a punchline, the world gets to shake.

Floating in rhythms, like jelly on toast,
We toast to the foolish, we revel the most.
With nerdy nicknames that tickle and leap,
In the arms of the whimsical, we dream without sleep.

Eternal shenanigans, we banter and play,
Where joy is the currency, laughter the way.
In the land of the silly, we'll never grow old,
With hugs from the cosmos, our stories unfold.

So let's dive in the laughter, let's splash in the fun,
Where the sparkles of timelessness shine like the sun.
In this embrace of the unmortal, we'll sway and we'll sing,
Laughing in circles, forever we spring.

The Legacy of Sweetness

In a vineyard where laughter can sprout,
Grapes gossip about what they're all about.
The juiciest tales, they roll with a wink,
Sipping on sunlight, they giggle and blink.

Beneath every leaf is a joke so divine,
The plump little fruits share old tales of wine.
They chuckle at barrels, where secrets reside,
And dance with the moonshine, their joy amplified.

With every sweet drop, they toast to the sun,
As bees buzz around, enjoying the fun.
The legacy lives in their sugary cheer,
A sip of sweet laughter, let's raise it—oh dear!

So next time you sip, remember the jest,
In the heart of the vineyard, they've crafted their best.
For life is a banquet, with flavors so fine,
And sweetness is laughter, poured softly like wine.

Glimmering Tides of Time

In vineyards where whispers of sunsets appear,
The grapes gather round, sharing humor and cheer.
They bob in the breeze, like sailors at sea,
Holding their breath for the next funny spree.

As shadows grow long, they plot with delight,
To sneak past the moon, in the deep of the night.
With each little giggle, they ripple like waves,
A treasure of joy, in sweet moments they crave.

With glimmers of starlight, they shimmer and shine,
Winking at passersby, plotting the divine.
For every old grape has a story or two,
Of daring adventures, and mischief anew.

So if you should wander through rows of delight,
Remember the spirits who dance in the light.
The glimmering tides will carry their rhyme,
In laughter and joy, they defy the harsh time.

Harvest Moon Dreams

Under a moon that hangs so round,
Grapes whisper secrets, a magical sound.
They dream of adventures, both silly and grand,
Picturing worlds where the oddest things stand.

With stems intertwined, they giggle and play,
Creating wild tales to brighten the day.
Each drop of sweet nectar, a giggle of glee,
Moonlight reflections on grapes set them free.

They dance with the crickets, toast to the night,
As shadows leap forward in the pale silver light.
Their dreams float like bubbles, so cheerful and bright,
While troubles are left in the morn's early sight.

So let the harvest moon shine on this harvest,
With laughter and joy, we'll crown it the best.
For every sweet grape has a dream to impart,
In the heart of the vineyard, where laughter's an art.

Whispers Beneath the Canopy

Beneath the great leaves where the soft shadows play,
Grapes spin their tales in the most humorous way.
They share silly stories of birds on the run,
Laughing at squirrels who think they're so fun.

With each gentle sway, they whisper in glee,
Sharing fond memories of the bumblebee.
Their laughter erupts like a bubbling brook,
In the canopy's embrace, there's joy to unhook.

When there's no one around, they giggle quite loud,
Bantering freely, their quirks make them proud.
For life is a game with each twist and each turn,
And until it's all harvested, they'll laugh and they'll yearn.

So next time you stroll through the vines lush and neat,
Listen closely to secrets that bring joy, oh so sweet.
For under the canopy where whispers combine,
Lies a treasure of laughter, the heart of the vine.

Sips of Cosmic Time

In the realm of clinking glasses,
Time sips sweet, not a drop passes.
Stars gather round for a grapevine dance,
With every swirl, they take a chance.

A galactic toast to outer space,
Where comets trip and meteors race.
Bottled laughter floats on cosmic breeze,
As planets wobble down to their knees.

Saturn's rings giggle, wear a hat,
Mars jokes it's single, imagine that!
With every sip, the universe sways,
Time's a jester in this wobbly maze.

So raise your glass, let the fun unfold,
In cosmic vineyards, stories retold.
With each clink, let the hilarity flow,
In the laughter of stars, we find our glow.

Vineyards Beyond Tomorrow

In vineyards tucked where shadows play,
Grapes giggle softly at the end of day.
Tomorrow's harvest, a whimsical sight,
Dancing in sunlight, oh what a delight!

A bunch in a beret, one with a tie,
Discussing philosophy and the why.
"Why do we hang?" one grape will say,
"Just to be plucked and whisked away!"

The sun chuckles, casting its glow,
As grapevines whisper secrets below.
With humor steeped in every vine,
Every sip is a punchline, divine!

So let's toast to sunbeams and mirth,
In this absurdly fantastic turf.
Here's to vineyards, where laughter is sown,
In a future where joy has truly grown.

Ripe with Remembrance

Beneath the trellis, memories vine,
Each one a giggle, a splash of wine.
Old grapes gossip, their tales entwine,
"Remember that time?" Oh, it's so fine!

A vintage joke from centuries past,
The fruitiest laughter, unsurpassed.
It ripened in barrels, stored with care,
A bottle of whimsy we love to share.

With every pop, a chuckle erupts,
As the cork flies high, like it's giving up.
History's served on a platter of fun,
Time's a clown, always on the run!

So raise your glass to nostalgia's cheer,
For every grape offers laughter here.
Ripe with remembrance, let's sip and see,
The joy of the past in eternity!

Vintage Echoes

In a cellar deep with dust and cheer,
Wine bottles whisper; lend an ear!
They share tall tales that tickle your nose,
The laughter of grapes as the history grows.

A vintage echo, a hiccup in time,
Reminding us all that life can rhyme.
With every sip, the stories unwind,
The punchlines pop in each drop you find.

"Remember that harvest?" one bottle will grin,
"When we went dancing with the moonlit kin?"
The corks all chuckle, the sediment sways,
In a symphony of giggles, it plays.

So join the chorus, let your heart leap,
In the vintage echoes that shuffle and creep.
Here's to the stories, the fun, and the cheer,
In the corked-up cosmos, forever near!

Beyond the Fading Light

In a field where shadows play,
A squirrel holds a grape bouquet.
He twirls with glee, a furry king,
Declaring fruity joy, let's sing!

The harvest moon, a giant pie,
Makes us wish we could just fly.
With every step, we laugh and trip,
Stumbling with our grape-filled grip!

Beneath the stars, we dance so free,
Each berry laughs, "Come laugh with me!"
The joy is ripe, the night's a show,
As grapes converse in whispers low.

So raise a toast, let's drink the night,
To squirrels, laughter, and pure delight.
A love of fruit, dreams take their flight,
Forever feasting in fading light.

Siren Songs of the Fruit

A grape once sang in a high-pitched tone,
"Come dance with me, you're not alone!"
The pears rolled their eyes, the apples sighed,
But the melon warned, "You can't abide!"

With each sweet note, the fruits took flight,
Bananas flipped, what a silly sight!
The citrus choir joined in the fray,
Swaying and singing till the break of day.

A fruit salad ball, a wobbly scene,
Strawberries spun in a glossy sheen.
With laughter that echoed beyond the grove,
Our twig-topped friends put on a show!

And when the sun crested, laughter waned,
The singing ended, but joy remained.
In every bite, that sweet refrain,
Forever marked by fruit's campaign.

Echoing Through the Vineyards

In a vineyard full of cheerful sights,
Grapes chuckle under twinkling lights.
With playful jests, they roll and bounce,
Each vineyard twist, a merry flounce.

The wind squeals jokes through leafy boughs,
As beetles giggle and ancient cows.
"Drink up, my friends!" the vines declare,
"Tomorrow's worries? Don't you dare!"

A cork pops loud, the laughter swells,
Each vintage tale that memory tells.
With every sip, old gripes retreat,
As we all dance to this grape-timed beat.

So through the rows of growing cheer,
Echoes of laughter, bright and clear.
The fruits of joy, a vineyard spree,
In grape-filled dreams, we all agree.

Tasting the Infinite

A grape of wisdom, round and sweet,
Said, "Join me, friend, we're in for a treat!"
With every bite, the world will spin,
And moments tasted will make you grin.

We search for paths that twist and bend,
Through every harvest, laughter blends.
Grapes spin tales on a sugary breeze,
While bees take notes on stanzas with ease.

With flavors dancing across our tongues,
We'll keep on laughing; we'll stay young!
A banquet laid under moonlit skies,
An endless feast where joy complies.

So let's drink deep from life's delight,
And taste the boundless with all our might.
For every grape holds a vibrant key,
Unlocking laughter, wild and free!